Room · Ystafell · Phòng

Parthian, Cardigan SA43 1ED
www.parthianbooks.com
First published in 2023
© 2023 The contributors
ISBN 978-1-914595-89-9
Editor: Joshua Jones
Cover Design by Syncopated Pandemonium
Cover photo by Joshua Jones
Typeset by Syncopated Pandemonium
Printed by 4edge
Published and developed with the support of the British Council
Wales as part of the UK/Viet Nam season.

Room · Ystafell · Phòng

Xuân Tùng, Joshua Jones, Kai Nguyễn, Leo Drayton, Maik Cây and Lauren Morais

PARTHIAN

Published and developed with the support of the British
Council Wales as part of the UK/Viet Nam season

Contents

It began to rain while Kai was giving me a ride back to my hotel on the back of his motorbike. My last night in Việt Nam. All around me the beeping horns fought for auditory dominance with the rain. As we passed over the river, I held onto his shoulders, and looked up at the sky.

Introduction

I sat on the outside of the table, drinking beers with two girls – 1 Spanish, 1 Italian – I had met mere hours ago, when it began to rain. I leaned out from underneath the red canopy, heavy with the thick droplets dropping hard, and I looked up at the sky, like I was about to insert contact lenses. The rain, I ran it over my scalp, pleasured the soak of my t-shirt that became transparent, showing the ghostly, wet skin beneath. I lit a cigarette. *I've missed the rain*, I said to my new friends who remained dry on the other side of the table. It reminds me of home.

There isn't exactly a suite of similarity between Welsh and Vietnamese rain in the spring. In Há Nội, it hadn't rained for days – or a couple of weeks even, according to some of the locals – so this first rain brought down the dust and pollution. All the stuff the thousands of motorbikes chuck up into the atmosphere every day. The next morning, realising my t-shirt, which I hung over the bottom of my bed in the hostel, smelt particularly funky, I washed it in the communal shower. The rain here was heavy, and the heat remained oppressive. Welsh rain feels fresh, clears the air. Or, it shrouds the air, a light mist embracing you as you walk through it.

I was miles away from anything I knew, and desperate to find familiarity anywhere I could. I got on with Irish backpackers the most, the closest I got to an accent like mine.

I didn't tell anyone I was queer, or autistic. Because I felt I had to protect myself — a feeling I hadn't experienced in a long time because of the social circles I've built around me in Cardiff. Although, I did, very drunkenly, tell my new Irish friend that my ex-boyfriend is transgender, and I love him still, and how much I hate transphobes. He said, aye, my cousin is transgender, and she's a laugh.

My time in Việt Nam, meeting artists and collectives in Há Nội and Ho Chi Minh City (Saigon), was full of firsts. First time outside of Europe, first time participating in a panel discussion on queer literature – one of the first events in Việt Nam of its kind – first time I truly saw how literature has the power to both bring together and comfort people. First time on the back of a motorbike, first time eating olives and enjoying them. First time I've been the only white person in a café, supermarket, neighbourhood, first time witnessing how queers in a different country, with a very different history and culture, mobilise and fight for their right to simply exist.

I personally chose who would join me in this project, Room/Ystafell/Phòng, by hand. Kai, Lauren, Leo, Maik, Tùng – photographers, playwrights, poets, actors, dancers. Like the queers of the past, I wanted to create a family. A chosen family of creatives to build a space with, in which we were safe to express ourselves with truth and acceptance. We explored the boundaries of language, gender and the hinterlands of the body, queerness within urban and/versus rural landscapes. We found commonalities within our experiences while also worrying about censorship in all its forms – whether from government, our families/environments, or from ourselves.

From drag and ballroom culture to queer media, to a

first kiss in a Cardiff nightclub, to queer dreamscapes, ecology and celebrating transgender experiences, this anthology of work is diverse in its form as well as content. I hope it'll light a fire in every young, scared queer's heart. I hope it'll show queer people that, wherever they are in the world, there is a family ready to accept them – even if you build that family yourself, from the ground up.

Joshua (he/him): Before we look at dictionary definitions, theories and what other people have to say. I'd like to hear what YOUR definition of queer is. Could you all share your personal definition/idea of what queer is below.

Leo Drayton (he/him): To me it means community and to be free from the binary norms

Tùng: I still think to be queer is just to be.
And that definition can accommodate so many things. The art circle I know of is very queer
being a monk is also very queer, for example.

Maik Cây: I think queer can be anything that is out of the heteronormative (or neurotypical eventuality)
codes of living (life?)

Tùng: I agree chị ơi. To build on both of our thoughts, to be queer is a protest against the entanglement of norms that forces us to be something else

Joshua (he/him): For me, queer is weird, other. To celebrate outsiderness. Queer is more than a lifestyle, an attitude. It's a

5

way of being. It encompasses gender, sexuality, neurodivergence, my interest in art, music and culture. It touches everything.

kaitotheninth: For me, sometimes it's the silence, or unexplainable, I've been struggling to
talk to people essentially who's close to me/
Sometimes it's the awkwardness of silence

Joshua (he/him): Yes, I agree.

Maik Cây: Agree x100. Being queer is being the other and surviving all the trials and traumas against being
the other.

Joshua (he/him): It's hard to relate, because that silence and that unexplainable would be completely different for everyone. But I know what you mean.

When the awkwardness of silence feels physical.

Maik Cây:
But also, I think, queer is love.
What we have here today as a tiny community is love

Xuân Tùng

Close all the doors
And dampen the air up

To the sound of
clanging droplets
                    in nitrogen decay

As the cranked decibels
fades red,
through my vein
Just leave me   alone
                        in the meadow

of undisturbed canine
desire
to discover
small wonders.

Under my trampling feet,
blades of green
triumph
a thousand battles
I'm small and
humbled.

Tỏa bóng — The divine shade

My first time ever voguing in a club was one and a half years ago when Há nội stumbled, bleary-eyed, out from the ruins of the pandemic. It happened in a small social club, where expats and locals navigated the same slippery, beer-stained floor, everyone trying to move closer to the vinyl record sounds coming from the DJ deck – that irresistible magic that pulls people in every Friday night.

At the time, I was a culture journalist and 25 – the intersection where most of my friends were over their "party phase", yet I couldn't care less. I wanted to immerse myself in the environment that I was going to write about and, outside of that, I needed to experience it for myself – I had stories that I desperately wanted to tell and that words couldn't seem to deliver.

James Brown, Fela Kuti, and CHIC energised us. The dancers were electrified and the circle appeared naturally in the middle of the dance floor – the dancers started to strut. The sound snuck between my ribs and stabbed my heart. I wanted to jump in, I was leaning forward, but my feet were rooted to the floor. A thousand scenarios froze me on the outskirts of the circle but one small voice reminded me "but I have a story!" That was all I needed. I took the centre of the circle as Robin S. "show[ed] me love" through the loudspeaker, telling me which beat to catch so I could vogue like they did in 90s Harlem. A minute passed, maybe an eternity, and I emerged from my trance confused by the cheers and the thunderous applause.

———

I don't find it hard to be content. A good day of sun and light breezes might be just enough to be comfortable with my own existence. A cup of chè thập cẩm[1], then life is good. But then again, if contentment is that easy to find, why do I always want more? Real life seems to have everything for me – a straight-passing gay man, but at the same time it never feels enough. Theoretically, I can drop this "gay lifestyle" at any point and settle with a family like all my friends do. Yet at the same time, I know the ultimate promise of human contentment – a good job, a happily-ever-after nuclear family, simply would not happen to people like me.

As Blanca in the TV series *POSE* once said, while other girls live in the world of "possibly maybe", trans girls like her live in a world of "would not happen". They'd put on wedding gowns and wear a smile on their way to compete in "bridal realness" at a ballroom function in a basement somewhere in New York. To have themselves a happily ever after in a blink of an eye, when the lights are blinding and the cheers are deafening enough to put you in a trance.

Ballroom, the home of voguing and all kinds of "magic around the world", has been the space where queer marginalised people

———

1   A sweet liquid dish (chè) made from coconut milk with mixed beans (thập cẩm, or "anything").

find refuge, live their arts and find a sense of trance – one that is strong enough, you can feel it *through the video screen*. When the dolls[2] dance, they do it for themselves – more precisely, for the sake of losing themselves. But on the runway spotlight, giving themselves to the vogue gods also means giving a crumb or two of their divinity to the audiences.

"Let the music take over... Let the vogue spirit take over you"[3]

———

Hau dong ritual, the biggest and most flamboyant happening in the village, usually pops up in one day before vanishing back into thin air and out of all conversations. But that day, the temple by the tail end of the village, near the graveyard, came alive. People flowed in and out on top of sedge mats – colourful spaces for seating that were rolled out from the indoor altar to the street.

In the village's consistently torpid pace of life, few things can be so extravagant, upbeat and bizarre drum beats whirl, đàn nguyệt[4] strings croon; the chầu văn[5] warble divine psalms. In a corner, his head subtly shakes, his body twisting and turning to the sound, while his visage shines pure delight. The music is as if fuelling the medium – donning red ao dai, blue eyeliner, sharp red lips and a thick layer of white make-up covering a

---

2   Ballroom slang for trans women.
3   Icon Leiomy Maldonado Miyake-Mugler, when asked how to dance vogue correctly.
4   A two-stringed Vietnamese traditional musical instrument typically used in chầu văn ensembles and hầu đồng rituals.
5   Chầu văn singers, typically featured in hầu đồng rituals.

domineering pair of cheekbones – to diligently swirl the air around him with two silk veil fans on hands.

"Outlandishly gorgeous – where do you hail from?
Outlandishly gorgeous – it's Ms. Chin, freshly hailing from Song Temple!"

"I bow to you, your dance is amazing!", my mom, kowtowing on the ground, praises in unison with fellow village people at the ritual. Meanwhile, kids like us only wait for the medium to hear the god's callings, reach a basket full of small bills and candy, then bless us with handfuls of goodness tossed from above. Laughters, hollers, silk swirls and money flying for an eternity – until the psalms eventually have to end, returning the temple to its everyday state of timid silence.

Looking back, these rituals remain the most queer-adjacent thing I have witnessed during my 18 years at the village. Mediums, which a majority are men, find in the Mother Goddess religion a divine explanation for their queerness.

"It's not bê đê – not bê đê[6] at all, excuse your mouth. It's fate!", Cô Diện, a medium, on Facebook Live.

Not a usual queer, these mediums have a higher calling: Following the shades casted by the deities above, using them as a divine mirror to imagine and realise better selves – and to liven the mortal world with psalms and performances during the process. Leaving their bodies as vessels for the gods, the mediums – often called slurs on the street, become the most

---

6   Vietnamese slang for a gay man, oftentimes used negatively. Borrowed from French word *pédéraste*

pristine individuals, casting heavenly reflections on surrounding mortals.

As heard in Hầu đồng	As heard in Ballroom
"Con lạy cô, Con lạy chúa cô"	"Work sister, work queen"
"Cô xinh quá, Cô múa đẹp quá!"	"Your face is beat for the gods, your performance is ovah!"
"Cô về cô ban tài phát lộc cho chúng con!"	"You serve opulence and the children are eating it up!"

———

Yet, as with any queer space, the hầu đồng ritual nights proves ephemeral – memories of it are so fragile, sometimes I doubt if I had even lived it. The medium, the star of the night who brought every villager to their knees, only returns in my mom's stories as a cautionary tale of "that queer lifestyle" that her children should keep away from.

Now, growing up gay with its accompanying set of issues, I come back to the queer spiritual expert, expecting to find in spirituality a way out for my queer life. I found thầy Đức – Há Nội's most famous medium - in Nguyễn Trinh Thi's "Love Man Love Woman" (2007), but the visit only left me devastated.

The mediums, the vessels for the goddesses, still can't take pride in their life of divine euphoria. Thầy Đức had to hide his spiritual life away to go out and hook up for the sake of being loved. The divinity turns out to not be the panacea of their queer problems, but a mere safe corner for them to go and preserve their precious pieces of selves from the cruel world out there. Waking up from the highs of the performance, they are still left with the sobering loneliness that anyone – not just queer people – faces.

In this essay, I truly wish I could have presented queer spirituality as a utopia, where us queers can, together, make meaning out of this queer existence. Yet, in failing to do so, I have the chance to question my motivation: why am I seeking divine intervention for a truly mortal – more specifically, social and, consequently, political – state of affairs? We get lonely because the heterosexual, patriarchal world actively denies us seats at the table. The beatdown makes us peculiar and out-of-this-world, but *if* we could, we would still prefer having a ***choice*** to live, breathe, and grind our feet down on this veritable real world.

———

In ballroom culture, some queens have pointed out that the balls, transcendental and life-saving as they are, cannot afford us the whole answer. One of them is the legendary house mother Dorian Corey, known for her appearance in Jenny Livingston's 1990 documentary *Paris is Burning*. "Refusing to allow the 'queen' to be Othered, [Corey] conveys the message that in **all of us** resides that longing to transcend the boundaries of self, to be glorified."[7]

"… Corey stresses that one can only learn to love the self when one breaks through illusion and faces reality, not by escaping into fantasy. Emphasising that the point is not to give us fantasy but to recognize its limitations, one must distinguish the place

7   From bell hooks' review of the documentary, "Is Paris Burning?"

of fantasy in ritualised play from the use of fantasy as a means of escape. (...) Corey encourages using the imagination creatively to enhance one's capacity to live more fully in a world beyond fantasy." – bell hooks, "Is Paris Burning?"

For some fortunate queer people, to have a home in the mystic is to find a way into an oasis, abundant and nurturing, after being forsaken in the vast nothingness, without any support or guidance. There, the ritualistic plays make us stars and spectacles. But, is it our job to be stars and spectacles? To burn bright 24/7 for a consumptive and voyeuristic audience, who love the light but want to distance themselves from the light sources, is simply exhausting. Why is it that the mystic and exotic is the only choice of place where us queers can feel love and fulfilment? When the electric vogue beats, or the gleeful châu văn psalms end, I want us to be radical enough to love – ourselves first, then the world – too. After transcending through thousands of fantastical planes of existence, I believe we hold enough power to find refuge in "island of selves" – a humble nirvana as described by Thích Nhất Hạnh, where the responses welling up from the silence within, then, *A profound shift occurs in your relations with others and the world around you.*

Lauren Morais

Concrete Jungle

'I heard you want to kiss me'.
I dared the devil
then,

St Mary's street,
twenty years old.
In Kongs den—
red lights, littered
our lips,
the mirrorball bled,
eyes ignited. I couldn't think
of them as pairs
the white tiles twitched,
this is it. I was ready set
my debut, my debt
Closing in, closer
than to a boy I could ever get,
remembering the recoil
in my membrane of all the men I met.

On Cardiff streets, sixteen,
kicking my feet,
Corroding while friends caressed.

Their adolescence was heaven sent,
while my essence was hell
bent, queer
beneath and bubbling, but
beyond reach
then.

Now,
I'm twenty
coming out
in Kongs den
thinking I'll climb
the skyscraper
and scream my being—

but i could only just about kiss her then.

My Cymru, My Heart

Cenedl heb iaith, Cenedl heb galon.
A nation without language, is a nation without heart.

But, what does it mean for my heart, my calon
in a nation without the words to describe it.
Does it beat, pulse or pitter patter
or tease with the sound of falling petals?
Does it sound at all?
When there's desperate ditch beyond my lips
just to mention,
I have a girlfriend.
There's no such word in Welsh.
What does it mean for my heart, my calon
if I can't describe what's in it?
Her.
When I can't speak the silver seed of my friend's soul
without calling him a man grabber. gwrywgydiwr.
He doesn't grab men.
He holds them as if they were dandelion orbs in his hands,
cherished.
He doesn't even make a wish.
What does it mean for his heart, his calon
in a nation with a language that stamps

on his hands that dandelion feathers could bruise?
My calon, my heart
sits, swelling in a choir of singing ribs,
cloaked, delicately in melanin skin,
only to be described "creatively" as
lliw coffi,
coffee coloured.
In books for the eyes of babes,
we are y plant lliw coffee
the coffee-coloured kids.
What does it mean for our hearts, our calonau
nuzzled in skin
in a nation without the language
to recognise who we are?

I recognise Cymru's heart,
it swells sweetly in my mouth
as I say caru ti
to my daffodil loves.

And,
And as much I would *love, caru*, to follow Cymru's
calon,
I know, I need
to lead it.
bleed it damp and devoted until *my* blood bursts through its
capillaries,
so I can exist within it.

I *want* to exist within it.

'Developed during *Landing Bolts*, a Fio production'

Existing within it, a year on – thoughts of a 22-year-old Cardiff lesbian at 2am

A year on, I haven't lead much apart from my own life. I sometimes gargle guilt because of this. I've wobbled down Womanby Street many times with my worrying hands, and hers, tangled and tentative as dogs' noses. Although I know it's not worry I should have, I'm safe here, safer than most. Yet sometimes, I clutch at her hands as if my hand were a dragon's jaw. I'm charging down Queen Street with 'hot welsh gay' charred on my chest, forked tongue out and ready. I'm not sure why. I can count on my five claws the times I've endured any mention of 'lesbo' or 'dyke' or sickened eyes. I do feel safe. But I still feel that if a ladybird were to land on me, I would bruise. I imagine a swarm of them sometimes; leaving plum dot to dots, as I sit on a metal barbed bench outside of McDonalds. I look up at Aneurin Bevan's spear-like finger, sprinkled with pigeon shit and think... I must take things into my own hands. I trace my ladybird bruises and make a pretty picture. I wait for her. I think about how we whisper 'nos da, caru ti', 'nos ar ôl nos' in the nape of each other's neck. I think about queer people before us. I think about the things they wanted to say, but couldn't. I think about queer people now. I think about the note in my phone at 3:21am, an unsent ode of cariad composed on Clwb

Ifor Bach's floor. I think about how I didn't send it to her because I thought I was messy and too much. I vow to be messy and too much. I think about how I want to eat oranges with her because that's what poets do. I think about the colour orange.

I think about how a boy told me, when he walks home at night, he just thinks about things like – how moron means carrot in Welsh. Moron. I think about how ironic that is. I think about the many times I've walked home at night wondering if I would be a buried moron in a week's time. I think about how lucky I am. How I can kiss her on chippy lane without too much worry, if truth be told. How a year on, existing within it, I've led my life with love. With her.

Maik Cây:
I think we are all shaped and formed in different ways
by the heteronormative social construct. We hardly escape the
social hierarchy based on power, sexual orientation, etc. We live
by the established rules
of the world, but queer-ing means a line of flight
out of that system

Leo Drayton (He/Him): agree

Tùng: sometimes i think of hetero couples who had everything
as listed, then still cheat on each other.
Is it because they just want a way out like that?
(also just a rhetorical question :p)

Maik Cây: Maybe they are just horny people who get tired of
*monogamy haha

Maik Cây

A LETTER ABOUT THE TEN QUEER DREAMS

Bạch Mai, September 6

Dear Ms. Agnes Davies-Phạm,

I hope you will forgive me for this extremely late response. Indeed, I wanted to get back to you right away, but certain irritating events have taken place that made my head spin and forced me to postpone my replying. Last Wednesday, I had to defend myself to avoid being sent to Mai Hương Mental Hospital – they thought there was no way a lesbian artist hag like me would not go crazy at the age of 81. I'm not crazy. I am still able to live *completely* alone in my mountain house, in the Bạch Mai wood. But I'm not writing this letter to explain said incident.

I also am taken by surprise that Mrs. Davies-Phạm, your mother, did not write to me directly, but instead bothered you. I understand that you are no stranger to the 8-year relationship between me and your mother in the '90s. I'm regretful that our separation was so unpleasant, but I hope you convey to your mother that I always wish her peace and happiness, as she deserves, and I still miss her, in the long shadows that the setting sun cast upon our good memories.

Regarding your proposal (which I understand that you follow your mother's orders), as I have affirmed many times in my manifestos, essays, and creative works, I do not believe in privatisation. I refuse to sell my dreams, which were passed on orally to some audience members at the Saturn Group exhibition in 1994 (and were also passed down orally to your mother, due to our intimate relationship). I refuse to let my dreams, the vessels of my private and painful Cassandra complex, the muted concertos of my subconscious, become economic units in any capitalist political-economic system, or eventually become a complex symbol that would be gradually institutionalised, or worse, become one of the responses to the functionalism that remains, unsurprisingly, of exceeding popularity. I refuse to make you and your mother my business partners.

Dear Agnes, I must confess that there was a time when I thought your mother would be my life partner, and we would grow old together. Yet, the time we basked in happiness together was so limited. I did not hesitate to use our shared money and assets, as well as your mother's own, to carry out my insane artistic and literary programmes, along with those of my queer artist comrades, yet your mother never made a fuss about it. She must have believed in my preaching about anti-privatisation, and consequently, considered her private property as a type of common property that could be widely shared. Or maybe she was just too compassionate towards me. Nevertheless, I owe your mother a lot.

In denying you and Mrs. Davies-Phạm this sale, I shall bring up another suggestion: I will share with you my ten dreams. As a devotee of the I Ching, I have always wanted to write a book of divination in a literary way, and 'Thập-Quái-Mộng' (The Ten

Queer Dreams, also known as 'Thập-Quái-Công-Án' or The Ten Queer Koans) is part of or all of that book.

You can use it as a purely literary text to enjoy and amuse yourself, or consider it as a fortune-telling text, so that if you need it and believe it, it will always have an answer for you. Or else, as you mentioned in your letter, you can utilise it as a kind of psychedelic stimuli for the multidimensional intelligence your team are building. It's up to you, only, whether these dreams are presented as they are, intact, or become food for a larger digestive chain. No forms derived from them or interfered with by them, are allowed to be privatised and commercialised.

THẬP-QUÁI-MỘNG

(THE TEN QUEER DREAMS)

Dream 1: *I flew up among the upside-down houses in a great vault of red bricks. I kept flying out of that red-brick vault, and out of myself over and over again.*

Dream 2: *A strange woman and I stood in front of each other, naked, like one person and their shadow on both sides of the mirror. She looked at me and I looked at her. She turned into my lover, then turned into my mother, then turned into my three thousand ancestors, then turned into my daughter, then turned into my three thousand descendants, then turned into myself. I lightly touched the mirror and the mirror fell and turned into a lake. I looked into the lake and saw a man. He turned into my lover, then turned into my father, then turned into my three thousand ancestors, then turned into my son, then turned into my three thousand descendants, then turned into myself. I lightly touched the lake and the lake jumped up and turned into a gateless gate. I asked myself: "If there is no gate, how can I get through?"*

Dream 3: *After the apocalypse, I had the choice to go back to any point in the so-called historical process, and I always went back to the 27th, the day before the end of the world, and then just hung around at every subway station and harbour with the poor, ragged people there. My 27th gradually rotted away. On another*

27th day, I drank beer from a skull-cup taken from the Ghough's Cave in Somerset, which I had stolen from the museum, with a group of labourers whose faces had become mushy in my experience.

Dream 4: *I sat at a tea party, on a comma-shaped spaceship, with one of my great-grandchildren in the very distant future. We wore silver pants that rustled when we move. I found it extremely difficult to explain to them, and a cow, of dualistic concepts like man/woman or straight/queer. They howled: "But all is all!" One mushroom, however, told me that it had read about queer/cwiar, a word I used to describe myself, in a specialised sociology book at the library, under 'Schizophyllum'. I was deeply troubled and lost, but a stone comforted me by sitting still.*

Dream 5: *I went to pray to the four Holy Mothers for an answer to the question I was assigned to ask, but I had forgotten the question. These four Holy Mothers: one has thousands of penises and breasts and lumps on her body, one is smooth without penises, breasts, or lumps, one is many persons, and one is none. They were incubating a giant egg that was very flat, and about 9 metres long. While waiting for my question, they said I could sit and incubate the eggs with them. This is the egg that will give birth to the mythical tail-swallowing snake, and on that snake's tail are all these existences. I sat cross-legged on the egg, and I felt the death of all these existences pounding against my skin.*

Dream 6: *Time is born from a vowel W. This vowel is infinitely blue and has the opacity level of one.*

div {
* width: ∞px;*
* height: ∞px;*

background: #002FA7;
opacity: 1.0;
}

Dream 7: *I am the mother of an invisible yellow monkey, that I know because I am also an invisible yellow monkey. Troops of invisible yellow monkeys live in the ghosts of the felled forests where their ancestors lived and died. All invisible yellow monkeys, after death, will shed their invisible yellow shells and transform into a form similar to a human poem. This form can be recited and memorised, sungsang, and used to stimulate the senses by generating a corresponsive chemical chain reaction, but most of the time, its purpose is to be forgotten.*

Dream 8: *I sat next to the perfect nothingness and clapped one of my hands until it made a sound like smoke running across a rainy field in the late afternoon. I walked for a long time in the rain and wove both the smoke and the rain into a blanket. I crawled into the perfect nothingness, put on this blanket, and went to sleep. While sleeping, I dreamed that I asked myself, in the perfect nothingness, is there me or not?*

Dream 9: *I wandered in a tight, complex, muted-coloured, and infinite structure; in both hands, I carried a heavy mirror, the surface of which was rippling and water-like, but not liquid. To find my way, I continuously looked at this mirror, which reflected the ceiling of the structure, and walked on the floor of the structure. The mirror could also be understood as an open book, translating the language in which the structure was communicating to me. This communication was continuous and non-stop, causing me a lot of pain from post-communication trauma. However, the mirror* *could also be understood as an umbilical cord, and I needed the mirror to continue to exist and move within the structure.*

Dream 10: *In a very cramped birthing room, nine other creatures and I gave birth to a new architecture. This new architecture was labelled: 'asynchronous masterless replication; low latency'. I think this architecture was a butterfly, but obviously, it might not have been a butterfly, but just a dot.*

———

These ten dreams, as I mentioned, were transmitted orally, from me to other listeners. In addition to my desire to never privatise or commercialise them, may I ask that you, if communicating them to another human-format (like you), never document them as I did above, but use word of mouth only. Other forms of documentation are acceptable for non-human formats.

The last thing I want to bother you with, and hope that you will convey to your mother, is that last Wednesday, when I was released from the mental hospital, they also informed me that I had lung cancer, final stage. I have a lot of support, people, and substances, you know, to not feel pain anymore and continue to maintain life in the mountains. Nature is the only thing that tolerates my pathetic existence. I think death is a gift, which people often fumble with and don't know how to open. However, I have a faint hope that your mother will visit me at 16 Bạch Mai Village.

I thank you very much and wish you all the best!

(To your mother) Mewn cariad ac undod *(just like when we lived in Brecon together)*

Trần Bích Băng

<u>PS</u>: I sent you and your mother a few photos I took of the ducks near my house. Of these ducks, two male ducks have paired off and incubated together for almost a year (the eggs they stole, I'm afraid). I hope your mother is amused by the little news I delivered.

Joshua Jones

Mother / Lenin / Joyance

A boy's mother, weeping,
hair trailing scummy pond water—
ends algae dip-dyed, a botch job—
subtle breeze brushes twiggy locks
into the path of surface skaters.
My favourite word is a tut—
I find myself rubbing my belly
watching fathers
teach children their first murder.
To start, you tear up the body, you break it
into bits then offer it up for the ducks, little deities,
bloated little Jesus, the size of a shoe,
floating face-down.

Why is she crying?
You'd think she'd be over it by now.
A child's death, toy soldier.
His skin trapped in a stone prison,
preserved from raw air.
The unfiltered gaze
from men tearing newspaper into strips
to roll their chicken-scented cigarettes,
and mothers
yet to face the death of a child.

At the park, the other day,
I saw a mother's son choking on a bap.
The father slapped the boy's back
with an open palm.
She swiped his hand away, proceeded
with the Heimlich manoeuvre—
mothers are always right. So, she pumped
his chest with her closed fist
until out sprung the bready treat,
and the ducks were fed once more.

Maybe, her weeping is because—
just because. Or because
his body's grey
when he should be wearing colour
or because the cloth of butterfly wings
shroud his body, a purple breath's distance.
When he was a young statue, a snake
coiled his arm like a beautiful dream
with teeth. Man, his drama
must have been something.
On at least two occasions, he was stolen
and later found, disguised by bushes,
bedded in dirt.

What about the hands that have desired
the curve of his stone body—
hands speak when mouths cannot.
have I been watching too many Jarman films?
Or not enough—
Who stole him? Who had their way
with the young Pan? So many men

walk with their hands in their pockets.
I want to know what their hands say—
is the love line of their palm bent, like a widow's spine?
His face, oblivious, smiles to the sun, regardless.

One blink is a year. His palms are washed smooth.
Maybe that's why she weeps for him. The nights
he got disappeared, nights of not knowing.
His total lack of awareness.
Trauma cakes the stone like dried shit
that Welsh rain can't wash away.

It's so me to think about the end of things—
flowers, boyhood, the lifecycle of ducks—
when the sun is shining, the coffee is sweet
the dogs are friendly.
I have come to believe depression is incurable,
but that might be the depression talking.

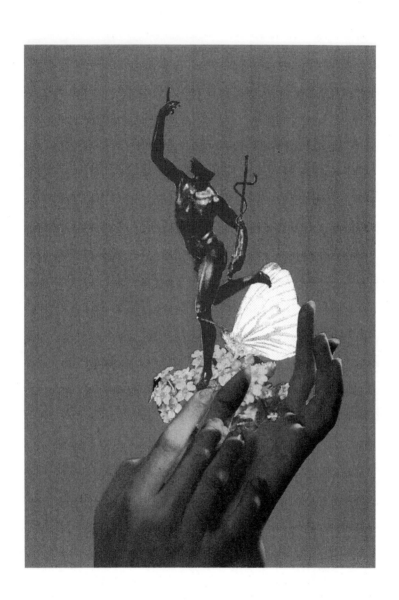

When, in Há Nội, I walked
and walked and looked
for men to photograph. To study.
Sleeping on the back of motorbikes,
under the shade of a wide-brimmed hat
or up on the roofs, installing their own wires.

When, in Há Nội, I felt the electric heat
leaning over a balcony,
in some hidden backyard,
I traced a finger along the vine
from a tree,
until I realised I was holding
a live wire.

When, in Há Nội, I watched a fisherman
wrestle a catch from the lake.
Held its head in the dirt until it stopped breathing,
His boy stood near, poised with a plastic bag.
They washed the grey thing with bottled water,
sold it to a smiling man, there and then.
I guess you can't get fresher than that.
I was so thrilled I forgot about my Cola,
flattening in the aching heat.

When, in Há Nội, I fell in love
with a reflection of myself.
The water was so still, so still, so—
quiet.
I didn't mind being stared at,
I was looking too.

When, in Há Nội, I saw the statue of Lenin
I thought I may have found a brother here.
But the government man
who'd followed me round the Old Quarter,
tapped me on the shoulder, told me to move on.

From boy to animal, being to object
the boy, is just a boy.
But also, a boy looking at a boy—
I am the boy. I am made of stone.
When I look at him I am looking
For... that three-letter word.
There's never a second magpie
when you want it.

I wanted to write a happy poem.
I really did. Almost.
This was going to be the one
where I let in the light.
Children blow bubbles at the boy
they burst upon the welcoming
finger, that says, look over
there. I'm always looking
over my shoulder, comrade.

The boy's name is joy. The young belly
looks good because it hasn't
touched a meal. Neither has mine.
He is smiling, he's happy, his penis
is a water faucet.
The waters, whatever the weather,
are cold. Birds perch on the end
of it, mistaking their nest
for ribs.

I wanted to write a happy poem.
Instead, I became birds.
Bloated, sap-drunk
from drinking willow's
weep. Scud running
over the heads
of men, lips
puckered towards
sky, to catch
the coppers
falling.

The natural progression, for a boy,
is to become a fountain.

kaitotheninth: what do you think of when you think of a queer environment @everyone?

laurenmorais: When I saw queer ecology I didn't think of space straight away I went to like queer relationships in the animal world and stuff, is that still a part of it

Joshua (he/him): No gods, no masters, no borders no fences, a self-governed space, a land that we move THROUGH, not against, or on top of
a space that appreciates aesthetical beauty in nature, and doesn't just see nature for gain, or to be consumed
A space that isn't owned

Leo Drayton (he/him): I rarely think of nature when talking about queer environments, i see bright lights, fabrics, people. sort of like the open mic art posters the other day, that's what i think of when talking about queer environment. the manmade environment the community built because there was no space anywhere else

Tùng: You're literally describing the Red River island ^^

its prob the only place in urban Há Nội that's not claimed by corporations

Joshua (he/him): love itttt

Tùng: People go there to find an escape from the city just inside the city, to bathe naked and reconnect with nature, do some meditation

Tùng: I feel like queer or not, we all dream of queer spaces
It's hard to be queer in the current pace of capitalism
so we all dream of places to be "more queer", even if you don't want to call it that

laurenmorais: I think very similar to Leo, also within that a freedom of expression of the self like when I'm in queer spaces I'm at my most comfortable, like I can breathe more easily – a breathable space I suppose ahaha I'm not sure what i picture, but at the moment it's a feeling if that makes sense

Joshua (he/him): makes perfect sense

Tùng: unclaimed land, unbridled by hierarchy and hegemony

Kai Nguyễn

burning season

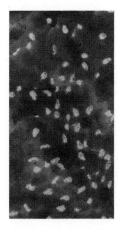

1. a broken pot, many-legged
insects shrivelling, writhing on the floor.
should a
heel touch a fallen piece, blood oozes

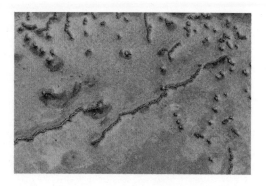

2.   elsewhere wind season, dry sand cooling
the soul at night, fragrant chinaberry
        flowers. the// flickering, burning cuts from the
reaped field, sweaty clumps of rice.
        I was running

        what people remember, what they forget,
memories flow vertically, refreshing

            traces of bruised flesh, which months and
days were etched on that
        tree. three years of drought, one of flood.

I was sinking in the heavy mist // far and distant
    uncertain who it belonged to

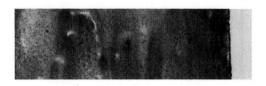

3. what I remember, what I
forget, the afternoons, engraving

your pale blue words
on// my flesh

sweat drips
down my spine

their tears

half of a naked foot
on red-hot coal

the smell of
burnt
flesh

my throat
stammering one-sided
exchanges

tôi đã mất giọng từ khi người...

mùa cháy

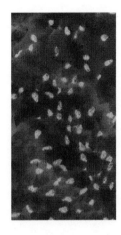

1. chậu cây vỡ, những con bọ nhiều chân quắt
   quéo trên sàn.
                     gót ai chạm một mảnh rơi, ướt máu

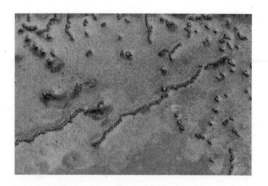

2. mùa gió một miền khác, cát khô rười rượi long
   bàn chân đêm, hoa
       xoan ngát. những // chập chờn, xót rát đồng
       gặt, bụi lúa bết mồ hôi. tôi chạy

người ta quên nhớ điều gì, ký ức chảy dọc, ướt mát

những vết thịt da xước xát, cây lá kia ghi khắc
những năm tháng
nào. ba năm hạn một năm lũ
 tôi chìm trong sương mờ // xa vắng
 không chắc của ai

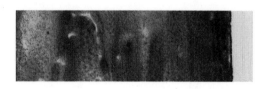

3. tôi quên nhớ gì những chiều hắn
 ên xanh xám
 chữ nghĩa người // thịt da tôi
 mồ hôi nhỏ giọt sống lưng
 nước mắt người

nửa bàn chân trần
 trên than đỏ

mùi da thịt
cháy

cổ họng mình ú ở những chèo kéo mượn vay
I've lost my voice since you

Leo Drayton

'Posing sodomite'

The world was my oyster, but I used the wrong fork.
Snacking on treats that weren't sweet enough for me.

Flamboyant!

buoyancy...

boys...

See me

performing for you even if you
hate the show.

I'll send you a free ticket to my trial if you'd like,
the more the merrier.
At least let me capitalise on my trauma.

Is sodomy still gay...

or have they stolen that too.

Take away my voice and I'll weaponize my words to fight against your blindness.

Pages steeped in metaphors your hatred will ignore.

I don't need your space when I can build my own

within words

worlds of pretty people

none as pretty as me.

Paint me

painting you.

Basil smells of Gray colours.

Colour me green
as the carnation on your lapel

Sell the dream of '*out and proud*' to those that understand
its meaning.

And one day the way we paved will dry.

My incarceration will amongst the last,

and our stories will not be metaphorical

anymore.

Rhosys Cochion

Gwelais ddyfyniad y diwrnod o'r blaen yn dweud nad oedd dynion yn debygol o dderbyn blodau nes y diwrnod y bu farw. Ac yma, wrth i mi eistedd a syllu ar fedd ffrind annwyl, a laddwyd drwy ddallbleidiaeth, sylweddolaf na dderbynnodd hi flodau cyn heddi chwaith. Efallai mae'n neges oddi wrth y byd yn dweud nad oedd hi yn fenyw eto. Rhesymeg ddiysgog... heb flodau = heb fenywdod. Fel dyn traws, galla i ddweud fy mod i wedyn derbyn blodau ac yn gobeithio na fyddaf byth eto. Dwi methu goddef yr arogl.

Mae yna rywbeth rhyfedd i mi am y syniad o dorri rhywbeth byw oddi ar wreiddiau'r peth sydd yn rhoi bywyd iddo a chyflwyno'r petalau darfodus fel anrheg i ffrind, yn gorfodu iddynt ei warchod a'i gadw'n fyw, gan wybod ei fod yn anochel y bydd y blodyn bach yn gwywo.

Mae yna ddywediad ym mysg llên draws sy'n dweud 'rhowch rosynnau i ni cyn i ni farw'. Dathlwch ein bywydau yn lle galaru'r marwlaethau dirifedi y gellid wedi eu hatal. Nad oedd y marwolaethau hyn yn anochel nes i'n gwreiddiau gael eu torri i ffwrdd. Felly, efallai yn hytrach na rhoi rhosys i ni, rowch ofal iechyd, cefnogaeth, buddsoddiadau ariannol... Bwydwch ein gwreiddiau fel y gallwn dyfu y tu hwnt i'n harddegau. Efallai wedyn na fyddaf yn eistedd yma gyda rhosys i ferch na fydd yn cael y cyfle i'w gwylio'n gwywo i ddim.

Red Roses

I saw a quote the other day about how men rarely receive flowers except on their graves. And as I sit here staring at the grave of a dear friend, murdered by bigotry, I realise that she never received flowers either. Maybe that's the world sending a message that she was not seen as a woman yet. It's hard to argue with that logic... no flowers = no womanhood. As a trans man I can say that I both have received flowers, and wished that I hadn't.

I can't stand the smell.

There's something strange to me about the idea of cutting away a living thing from the roots which give it life, then giving the decaying petals to a friend, forcing them to keep it alive as long as possible, but knowing they will inevitably wilt away.

There is a saying in trans lore that says

'give us our roses before we die'. Celebrate our lives instead of mourning countless deaths that could have been prevented. Those deaths were not inevitable until our roots were cut away. So, maybe, instead of giving us roses, give us healthcare, support, financial investments... Feed our roots so we can grow past our teen years. Maybe then I wouldn't be sitting here with roses for a girl who will never have the chance to watch them wilt away.

The notes app of a first-time Việt Nam traveller – Joshua Jones

Food & Drink

Banh mi — 5
Spring Rolls — 20
Summer rolls — 16
Há Nội-brand beer — 19
Saigon-brand beer — 11
Tiger, beer — 4
Coffee, black, w sugar — 15
Bottled water —
Croissants — 10
Watermelon, servings — 3
Pack of Marlboro Red (20) — 4
Pack of Marlboro Gold (20) — 3

Times I've (knowingly) broken veganism — 10 (croissants)
Sharing pack of paprika-flavoured crisps I've eaten on my own
— 4

Things Bought

Books — 9
H.G Wells, The Invisible Man

Haruki Murakami, Underground
John Berger & Jean Mohr, A Fortunate Man
Dan Hambleton, Warm Rain (book written by an expat living in Há Nội)
Ajar Press journal, issues 3-5
Minh Pham & Paola Boncompagni, Hanoi Hanoi (photography book)
Myan Tho & Hinh Anh, Movement
Invisible Space & Beautiful Noise, Ghost of Time Gone By
Nhã Thuyên, un/martyred

From Matca —
The rest is history
From Here On Out, 02
Scrapbook, 02
Teen Spirit
Postcards, pack of 4

Coaster, made by indigenous Vietnamese women, for my mother
Columbia-brand sunhat, black
North Face cargo trousers, black, 1 pair
Patagonia-brand t-shirt, black, 1
Enamel pin — 1 (of a frog)
Fujifilm 35mm film, ISO 200 — 2 rolls
Handmade notebook, rice paper — 1
Studio Ghibli postcards — 4
Bookmarks — 2
Stamps — 2 packs

Things Lost

Toiletry pack —

Toothbrush, 1
Toothpaste, 1 tub
Sunscreen, spf50 w moisturiser (face)
Sunscreen, spf50 (body)
Aftersun
Mitchums deodorant spray, 1

Fruit pastilles, 1 pack
1 enamel pin (later found)

Places Stayed

Little Town Hotel, Há Nội
Nexys Hostel, Há Nội
Air BnB, Há Nội
Riverside Hotel, Saigon

Misc

Times almost ran over —
7 (motorbike/moped)
2 (car)

Men I've wanted to kiss — 6
Women I've wanted to kiss — 5
People I've kissed — 0

Felt like an outsider — 6
Experienced anxiety (regardless of extremity) — 9

Times I was ripped off — 3

Poems written — 3
Photographs taken on Pentax MTL 5 camera — 72

Little dogs spotted — 26
Cats — 4
Dying kittens in a cage — 2
Birds in cages on the street — 23 (approx.)

Nationalities of People I've Met —

Australians, 5
New Zealanders, 2 (boring couple)
Netherlands, 1
Denmark, 1 (boring gamer bro)
Belgian, 4
Italian, 1
German, 2 (2 of them, guys, had nipple piercings)
French, 4
Irish, 3 (all of them, sound)
Canadians, 4
Americans, 2
English, 3
Scottish, 1 (shared fries)
Welsh, 0 (☹)

Biographies

Xuân Tùng (he/him) is a Há Nội-based writer and dance advocate. Focusing on investigative journalism and cultural criticism practices, his writing strives to make sense of social-cultural shifts and queerness in contemporary Vietnam.

Lauren Morais (she/her) is a poet and spoken word artist from Cardiff. She is currently one of the writers of Fran Wen's production of *Popeth Ar y Ddaear*. She also wrote a spoken word track with Sywel Nyw, which concentrated on the unsaid and the things that bubble on our tongues.

Maik Cây (she/her-they-them) is an independent writer, playwright, and filmmaker from Há Nội, Việt Nam. They are the co-founder of Tiếng-Thét, a queer, feminist creative group that works to promote marginalized voices of unheard local artists and writers.

Their work includes short film *As I lay dying* (2015), selected for screening at the 62nd International Short Film Festival Oberhausen, award-wining debut novella *Wittgenstein of the black paradise* (2018), and short plays *Blue monologue* (2020) and *The dreams of three lives* (2022), both of which produced for theatrical projects led by the Goethe-Institut Vietnam.

Joshua Jones (he/him) is a writer and artist from Llanelli, South Wales. He is the co-founder of Dyddiau Du, a social hub and community art-space for queer & neurodivergent people in Cardiff. His publications include *Fistful of Flowers* and his debut collection of short stories, *Local Fires*, was published by Parthian Books in November 2023.

Kai Nguyễn (he/him) is a multimedia artist based in Ho Chi Minh City. His practice focuses on the poetry of moving images, space, and plants. Kai's works are featured on AAWW, AJAR Press, The Factory Contemporary Arts Centre and Matca. In 2022, Kai co-founded 3năm Studio, a community arts space. From 2019 to 2022, Kai initiated Invisible Space, a community space for local young artists. During COVID-19 lockdowns, they created a collective diary called "Ghost of time gone by" as part of a 10-week online workshop series.

Leo Drayton (he/him) is a young poet and aspiring playwright and filmmaker from Cardiff. He was a cowriter on the Welsh language book series *Y Pump*. As a proud queer trans man, Leo is keen to create and share work about his identity.

Phương Anh (she/her) is a translator and writer from Vietnam, and currently doing cultural studies at University College London. Her work has been published on Asymptote, PR&TA, Modern Poetry in Translation, and SAND among others.

Translated *burning season* by Kai Nguyễn on page 59.

Rey Hope (he/they) is a neuroqueer environmentalist artist from South Devon, now living in Cardiff. They are the co-founder of Dyddiau Du and co-host of Cardiff Collage Club. He studied

Wildlife Ecology and Conservation Science at UWE Bristol and is now experimenting with combining art and environmental practices. Their creative work explores identity, place, queerness, disability, and nature through the mediums of collage, found and foraged objects.

His collage work is featured on page 46 and page 52.

PARTHIAN A Carnival of Voices

'For almost thirty years, [Parthian] have been one of the most consistently agile imprints in Wales.' –
Mike Parker, *Planet Magazine*

'From the selection of its authors and topics covered through to the editing and production of the books,
Parthian exudes quality. It puts out a dazzling, stimulating, thought-provoking selection of books on par
with (if not better and more interesting than) the bigger publishing houses.' – Jenny White, journalist

'a vital part of our publishing scene in Wales and great ambassador for the best of Welsh writing.' –
Rebecca Gould, Head of Arts at British Council Wales

We have always published first time fiction and aim to give new writers as much development support
as we can. Our recent success includes writers such as Richard Owain Roberts (Not the Booker Prize
winner 2020), Alys Conran (Wales Book of the Year winner 2017).Tristan Hughes (Edward Stanford
Travel Writing Award – Fiction with a Sense of Place winner 2018), Lloyd Markham (Betty Trask Award
winner 2018) and Glen James Brown (Orwell and Portico Prize shortlistee 2019).

An engagement with the culture of Wales through our Library of Wales series has reached fifty titles of
classic writing. The Library of Wales has been a ten-year publishing project with support from the Welsh
Government and the Welsh Books Council, and has seen an investment of over £500,000 in the literary
and educational culture of Wales, with sales approaching 100,000 copies across print and digital formats.
It has changed the perception of Welsh writing, with *Poetry 1900–2000*, a title commissioned by Parthian
for the series, being adopted onto the Welsh Joint Education GCSE English syllabus, while many of the
books are now studied at university level in Wales.

The Modern Wales series, a collaboration with The Rhys Davies Trust, takes a look at the recent history
of Wales. This includes the publication of major works of biography: *Rocking the Boat: Welsh Women who
Championed Equality 1840-1990* by Angela V John and *Labour Country: Political Radicalism and Social
Democracy in South Wales 1831 to 1985* by Daryl Leeworthy. The trust have committed to a three-year
investment in the series.

Our engagement strategy is to work collaboratively and look to develop new initiatives. We aim to
produce attractive and readable books in our areas of interest: new writing, the heart of Welsh culture
and a view to the wider world through our Parthian Carnival.

We also publish the Library of Wales series edited by Professor Dai Smith. The series includes books
such as *Border Country*, *The Black Parade* and Dannie Abse's *Ash on a Young Man's Sleeve*. Recent books
include *Dat's Love and Other Stories* by Leonora Brito, *In and Out of the Goldfish Bowl* by Rachel Trezise
and Booker Prize-longlisted author Stevie Davies's novel *The Element of Water*.

Over the years we have developed good translation links throughout Europe and beyond, and our books
have appeared in over thirty foreign-language editions including German, French, Italian, Spanish,
Arabic, Chinese, Danish, Turkish, Portuguese and Russian. New for 2021 was *The Blue Tent* by Richard
Gwyn in French and Gary Raymond's *The Golden Orphans* in Turkish and Arabic, and we signed a deal
with the Nigerian publisher Purple Shelves for Eric Ngalle's memoir.

We have also published a growing list of fiction in translation from European languages, which has
included novels translated from Basque, Latvian, Catalan, Czech, French, Slovakian and Turkish.
Most recently, we published a series of books with support from Creative Europe, with an investment
of £150,000 over three years and collaboration with the literature councils of five European countries
leading to eleven new books in translation from some of the smaller languages of the European Union,
including Greek, Danish and Irish.